~A BINGO BOOK~

Virginia
Bingo Book

COMPLETE BINGO GAME IN A BOOK

Written By Rebecca Stark

I0167374

ISBN 978-0-87386-539-5

Educational Books 'n' Bingo

Printed in the U.S.A.

DIRECTIONS

INCLUDED:

List of Terms

Templates for Additional Terms and Clues

2 Clues per Term

30 Unique Bingo Sheets (To cut out or copy)

Sheet of Markers (to copy and distribute)

1. **Either cut apart the book or make copies of ALL the sheets. You might want to make an extra copy of the clue sheets to use for introduction and review. Keep the sheets in an envelope for easy reuse.**

2. Cut apart the call sheets with terms and clues.

3. Pass out one bingo sheet per student. There are enough unique sheets for a class of 30.

4. Pass out the markers. You may cut apart the markers included in this book or use any other small items of your choice. Students can also mark the sheets themselves; recopy the sheets as needed for additional games.

5. Decide whether or not you will require the entire sheet to be filled. Requiring the entire sheet to be filled provides a better review. However, if you have a short time to fill, you may prefer to have them do the just the border or some other format. Tell the class before you begin what is required.

6. There are 50 terms. Read the list before you begin. If there are any terms that have not been covered in class, you may want to read to the students the term and clues before you begin.

7. There is a blank space in the middle of each sheet. You can instruct the students to use it as a free space or you can write in answers to cover terms not included. Of course, in this case you would create your own clues. (Templates provided.)

8. Shuffle the sheets and place them in a pile. Two or three clues are provided for each term. If you plan to play the game with the same group more than once, you might want to choose a different clue for each game. If not, you may choose to use more than one clue.

9. Be sure to keep the sheets you have used for the present game in a separate pile. When a student calls, "Bingo," he or she will have to verify that the correct answers are on his or her sheet AND that the markers were placed in response to the proper questions. Pull out the sheets that are on the student's sheet keeping them in the order they were used in the game. Read each clue as it was given and ask the student to identify the correct answer from his or her sheet.

10. If the student has the correct answers on the sheet AND has shown that they were marked in response to the *correct questions,* then that student is the winner and the game is over. If the student does not have the correct answers on the sheet OR he or she marked the answers in response to *the wrong questions,* then the game continues until there is a proper winner.

11. If you want to play again, reshuffle the sheets and begin again.

Have fun

TERMS

Appalachian Plateau

Atlantic Coastal Plain

Blue Ridge

Blue Ridge

Cape Henry Lighthouse

CIA

Charlottesville

Chesapeake Bay

Confederate States of America

County (-ies)

Jefferson Davis

Dogwood

Executive Branch

Flag

Patrick Henry

Industry

James River

Jamestown

Thomas Jefferson

James Madison

James Monroe

Judicial Branch

Robert E. Lee

Legislative Branch

Lewis and Clark

Monticello

Motto

Mount Rogers

Mount Vernon

Nickname

Norfolk

Pentagon

Piedmont

Pocahontas

Powhatan

Richmond

Roanoke Colony

Seal

Shenandoah Valley

John Smith

Tobacco

Nat Turner

Union

University of Virginia

Valley and Ridge

Virginia Plan

George Washington

West Virginia

Williamsburg

Yorktown

Additional Terms

Choose as many additional terms as you would like and write them in the squares. Repeat each as desired.
Cut out the squares and randomly distribute them to the class.
Instruct the students to place their square on the center space of their card.

Virginia Bingo

© Barbara M. Peller

Clues for
Additional Terms

Write two or three clues for each of your additional terms.

_____ 1. 2. 3.	_____ 1. 2. 3.
_____ 1. 2. 3.	_____ 1. 2. 3.
_____ 1. 2. 3.	_____ 1. 2. 3.

Virginia Bingo

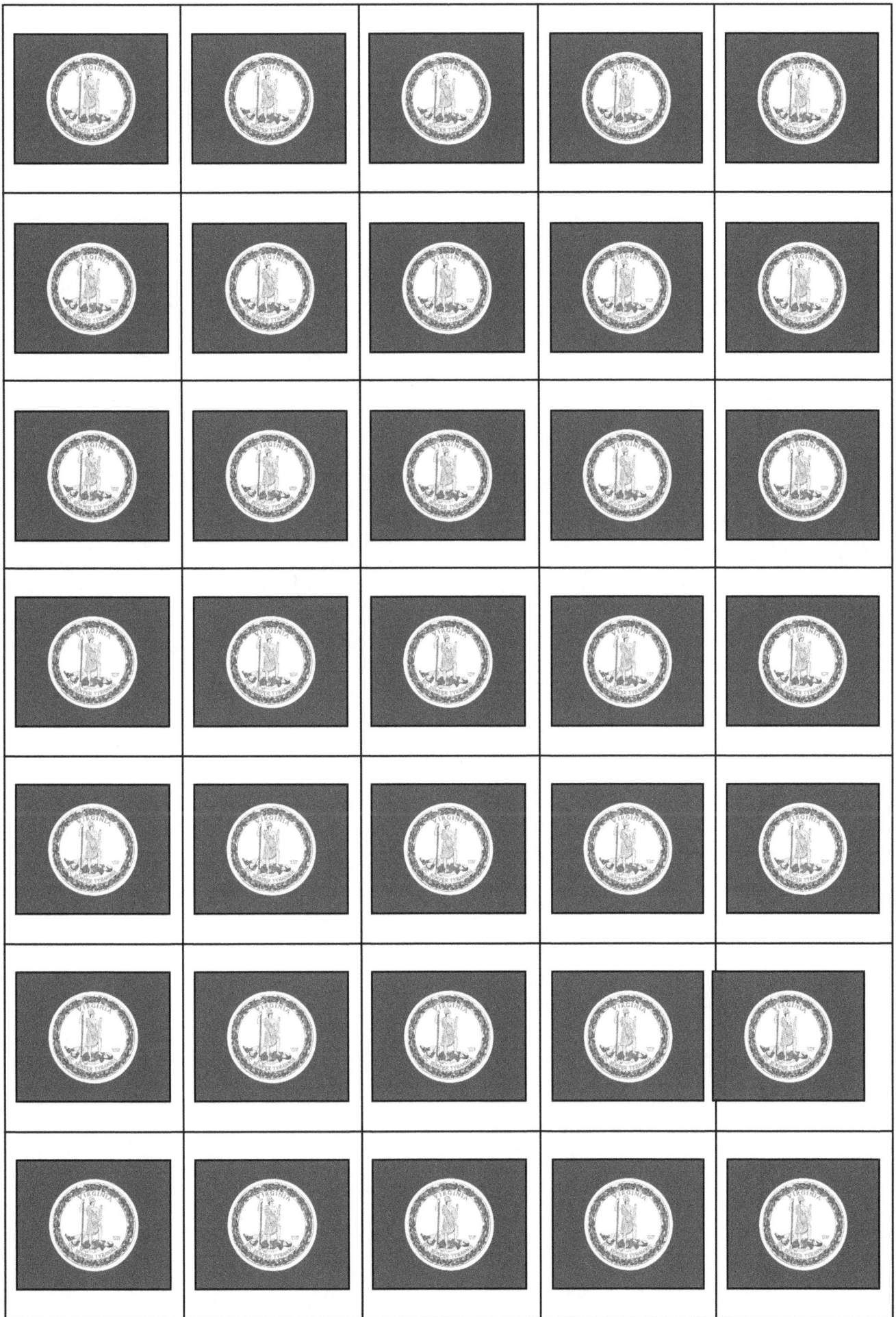

Appalachian Plateau

1. Coal mining is an important industry in this high plateau.

2. The ___ extends into Kentucky as the Cumberland Plateau.

Atlantic Coastal Plain

1. The ___ runs about 100 miles inland along the Atlantic Ocean. These lowlands are covered with salt marshes and swamps.

2. This region is often called the Tidewater. Jamestown, Williamsburg, and Yorktown are in this region.

Blue Ridge

1. The ___ Region is west of the Piedmont. Mount Rogers, the highest point in the state, is in this region.

2. The ___ Mountains are part of the Appalachian mountain system.

Border

1. West Virginia, Maryland, North Carolina, Tennessee, Kentucky, and the Atlantic Ocean all ___ Virginia.

2. Virginia forms the southwest ___ of Washington, DC.

Cape Henry Lighthouse

1. ___ was the first one to be erected by the federal government

2. The ___ is located on Virginia Beach.

CIA

1. ___ is an acronym for the Central Intelligence Agency.

2. The area in Virginia where headquarters of the ___ are located is known as Langley.

Charlottesville

1. ___ is best known as the home of two United States Presidents: Thomas Jefferson and James Monroe.

2. The University of Virginia is located here.

Chesapeake Bay

1. It is the largest estuary in the United States.

2. The Potomac, Rappahannock, York, and James rivers flow into the ___, creating three peninsulas.

Confederate States of America

1. The ___ was a government set up from 1861 to 1865.

2. Virginia was one of 11 states that seceded from the Union to form the ___.

County (-ies)

1. Virginia has 95 ___ and 39 independent cities.

2. Municipalities incorporated as cities are independent cities and are not part of any ___.

Jefferson Davis	Dogwood
1. ___ was the President of the Confederate States of America during the Civil War. 2. He and his family moved into the White House of the Confederacy in Richmond in May 1861.	1. The ___ is the official state tree. 2. The flower of the ___ is the official floral emblem of the state.
Executive Branch	**Flag**
1. The governor is head of the ___. The present-day head of this branch is [fill in]. 2. The ___ of government enforces laws. The governor, the lieutenant governor, the attorney general, and the governor's cabinet are part of this branch.	1. The ___ of the Commonwealth of Virginia has a blue field. 2. The state seal is centered on the ___ of the Commonwealth of Virginia.
Patrick Henry	**Industry**
1. He said, "Give me Liberty, or Give me Death!" in a speech he made to the Virginia Convention. 2. This Virginian Patriot was the first governor of the Commonwealth of Virginia.	1. Farming is an important ___ in the Piedmont and the Valley and Ridge regions. 2. Shipbuilding is an important ___ in the Atlantic Coastal Plain, or Tidewater.
James River	**Jamestown**
1. The ___ is the nation's largest river that is entirely within one state. 2. Native Americans in the region called this river the Powhatan River after the chief of the Powhatan Confederacy.	1. Founded in 1607, ___ was the first permanent English settlement in what is now the United States. 2. After Captain John Smith left ___, the colonists endured a period of starvation.
Thomas Jefferson	**James Madison**
1. This Virginian was the main author of the Declaration of Independence. 2. ___ was the first secretary of state, the second Vice-President and the third President of the United States.	1. ___ is called the "Father of the Constitution." 2. This Virginian was the fourth President of the United States.

Virginia Bingo

James Monroe

1. This Virginian was the fifth President of the United States.

2. His doctrine put forth in 1823 warned European nations not to get involved in political matters in Central and South America.

Judicial Branch

1. The ___ interprets what our laws mean and makes decisions about the laws and those who break them.

2. The ___ is made up of several courts, the highest of which is the state Supreme Court.

Robert E. Lee

1. ___ commanded the Confederate Army during the Civil War.

2. ___ surrendered to General Grant at Appomattox Court House on April 9, 1865.

Legislative Branch

1. The General Assembly is the ___ of government; it comprises the Senate and the House of Delegates.

2. The ___ of government makes the laws.

Lewis and Clark

1. The ___ Expedition was led by Meriwether Lewis, who was born in Albemarle County.

2. William Clark, who co-captained the ___ Expedition, was born in Caroline County, Virginia.

Monticello

1. ___ was the plantation home of Thomas Jefferson, who designed it.

2. Located just outside Charlottesville in the Piedmont region, this plantation was originally 5,000 acres.

Motto

1. *"Sic Semper Tyrannis"* is the state ___. It means "Thus always to tyrants."

2. The state ___ is on the state seal below the picture of the Roman goddess Virtus.

Mount Rogers

1. The highest natural point in the state is ___ at 5,729 feet.

2. ___, the highest natural point in the state, is in the Blue Ridge Mountains in Grayson and Smyth counties.

Mount Vernon

1. ___ was George and Martha Washington's home for more than 40 years.

2. Situated along the Potomac River in Northern Virginia, ___ is 16 miles south of Washington, DC.

Nickname

1. Old Dominion is the official ___ of Virginia.

2. Another ___ for Virginia is "Mother of Presidents" because it is the birthplace of 8 U.S. Presidents: Washington, Jefferson, Madison, Monroe, Harrison, Tyler, Taylor and Wilson.

Virginia Bingo

Norfolk 1. ___ is the second largest city in Virginia. The first largest is its neighbor Virginia Beach. 2. A naval station is located in ___.	**Pentagon** 1. The ___ is headquarters of the United States Department of Defense. It is in Arlington County. 2. The ___ is sometimes used to refer to the Department of Defense itself rather than the building.
Piedmont 1. The ___ Region is west of the Atlantic Coastal Plain and east of the Blue Ridge Mountains. It is the state's largest geographical land region. 2. Appomattox and Monticello are in this region.	**Pocahontas** 1. ___ was the daughter of Powhatan, chief of the Algonquian Indians. 2. She married tobacco planter John Rolfe.
Powhatan 1. He was chief of the the Algonquian Indians in the Chesapeake Bay area of Virginia. 2. His daughter married tobacco planter John Rolfe.	**Richmond** 1. This independent city is the capital of Virginia. 2. ___ was capital of the Confederate States of America.
Roanoke Colony 1. Sir Walter Raleigh's first expedition to ___ in 1585 failed, but he sent a second in 1587 with a larger group of settlers. 2. The colonists of ___ disappeared. The only clue was the carving on two tree trunks: CROATOAN and CRO.	**Seal** 1. The Great ___ of the Commonwealth features the Roman goddess Virtus standing over a defeated opponent. 2. Beneath the representation of Virtus on the Great ___ is the state motto, *Sic Semper Tyrannis.*
Shenandoah Valley 1. ___ stretches 200 miles across the Blue Ridge and Allegheny mountains. There are many caverns here, including Luray Caverns. 2. ___ is in the series of valleys known as The Great Valley of Virginia.	**John Smith** 1. Captain ___ became Jamestown's leader in 1608; he established a "no work, no food" policy. 2. Jamestown leader ___ was instrumental in trading with the Powhatan Indians for food.

Tobacco 1. John Rolfe's Virginia ___, called "Orinoco," became an important cash crop. 2. ___ is still an important crop of the Piedmont.	**Nat Turner** 1. The ___ Rebellion was a slave rebellion that took place in Southampton County, Virginia, in August 1831. 2. An eclipse of the sun convinced ___ that it was a supernatural sign from God to start an insurrection.
Union 1. The Commonwealth of Virginia became the tenth state to join the ___ in 1888. 2. Virginia voted to secede from the ___ on April 17, 1861, after the Battle of Fort Sumter.	**University of Virginia** 1. The ___ was founded by Thomas Jefferson in 1819. 2. It is the only university to be founded by a President of the United States.
Valley and Ridge 1. The ___ Region is west of the Blue Ridge Mountains and east of the Allegheny Mountains. There are many caverns in this region. 2. The Great Valley of Virginia lies against the Blue Ridge in the eastern part of this region.	**Virginia Plan** 1. The ___ was a proposal by Virginia delegates to the Constitutional Convention of 1787 for a bicameral, or 2-chamber, legislative branch. 2. The ___ set forth the idea for representation based upon population in the natonal legislature.
George Washington 1. This Virginian was commander-in-chief of the Continental Army during the American Revolutionary War. 2. This Virginian was the first President of the United States of America.	**West Virginia** 1. ___ became a state when it broke away from Virginia during the American Civil War. 2. ___ was the only state to form by seceding from a Confederate state.
Williamsburg 1. The College of William and Mary, the 2nd-oldest institution of higher education in the United States, is located in ___. 2. ___ became the capital of Colonial Virginia in 1705.	**Yorktown** 1. On October 19, 1781, General Cornwallis surrendered at ___. 2. Although the war would last for another year, this British defeat at ___ effectively ended the American Revolution.

Virginia Bingo

Virginia Bingo

Legislative Branch	Judicial Branch	Lewis and Clark	Yorktown	George Washington
Confederate States of America	Atlantic Coastal Plain	Williamsburg	Norfolk	Robert E. Lee
Nat Turner	Roanoke Colony		Monticello	Pocahontas
Virginia Plan	Cape Henry Lighthouse	James Madison	University of Virginia	Motto
Mount Rogers	County (-ies)	Executive Branch	Jamestown	James Monroe

Virginia Bingo: Card No. 1

Virginia Bingo

Virginia Plan	Union	Mount Vernon	Richmond	Mount Rogers
Motto	Norfolk	Charlottesville	Cape Henry Lighthouse	Tobacco
Shenandoah Valley	County (-ies)		Flag	James Madison
Border(s)	John Smith	Roanoke Colony	Piedmont	Robert E. Lee
James Monroe	Williamsburg	Executive Branch	Confederate States of America	Jamestown

Virginia Bingo

Virginia Plan	James Madison	Norfolk	University of Virginia	Nat Turner
County (-ies)	Atlantic Coastal Plain	Thomas Jefferson	Judicial Branch	Pentagon
Cape Henry Lighthouse	Williamsburg		Tobacco	Patrick Henry
Roanoke Colony	Shenandoah Valley	Mount Rogers	Jamestown	Mount Vernon
Blue Ridge	Confederate States of America	Executive Branch	Piedmont	Lewis and Clark

© Barbara M. Peller

Virginia Bingo

Roanoke Colony	Tobacco	Mount Rogers	Confederate States of America	Lewis and Clark
Nickname	Charlottesville	Judicial Branch	Richmond	Nat Turner
Monticello	Jamestown		George Washington	Yorktown
James Madison	Patrick Henry	Williamsburg	Executive Branch	Blue Ridge
Industry	James Monroe	Powhatan	Thomas Jefferson	Pocahontas

Virginia Bingo: Card No. 4

Virginia Bingo

James Monroe	George Washington	Cape Henry Lighthouse	Charlottesville	Confederate States of America
Nickname	James Madison	Border(s)	Flag	Atlantic Coastal Plain
Union	Pocahontas		Jamestown	Dogwood
Robert E. Lee	Tobacco	Legislative Branch	Piedmont	Industry
Norfolk	Executive Branch	Seal	Roanoke Colony	Monticello

Virginia Bingo: Card No. 5

Virginia Bingo

Border(s)	Tobacco	Mount Vernon	Union	Pocahontas
University of Virginia	Cape Henry Lighthouse	Industry	Judicial Branch	Nat Turner
Richmond	Jamestown		Charlottesville	Flag
Executive Branch	Mount Rogers	Piedmont	Powhatan	Monticello
Motto	James Madison	Legislative Branch	Seal	Lewis and Clark

Virginia Bingo: Card No. 6

Virginia Bingo

Legislative Branch	Tobacco	Dogwood	Thomas Jefferson	Norfolk
Motto	Lewis and Clark	County (-ies)	Jamestown	Nickname
Mount Vernon	Yorktown		Flag	Jefferson Davis
Roanoke Colony	James River	Nat Turner	Virginia Plan	Shenandoah Valley
Executive Branch	Confederate States of America	Piedmont	Powhatan	Border(s)

Virginia Bingo: Card No. 7

Virginia Bingo

Monticello	Tobacco	CIA	University of Virginia	Jefferson Davis
Nickname	Union	Richmond	Pocahontas	Charlottesville
Nat Turner	Appalachian Plateau		Lewis and Clark	George Washington
Jamestown	Roanoke Colony	Virginia Plan	Industry	Border(s)
Williamsburg	Executive Branch	Powhatan	Cape Henry Lighthouse	Motto

Virginia Bingo

Flag	Norfolk	County (-ies)	Nat Turner	Pocahontas
Industry	Union	Monticello	Cape Henry Lighthouse	Lewis and Clark
Pentagon	Legislative Branch		Atlantic Coastal Plain	CIA
Jefferson Davis	James Monroe	Mount Rogers	James River	Dogwood
Thomas Jefferson	Piedmont	Patrick Henry	Virginia Plan	George Washington

Virginia Bingo

Virginia Plan	University of Virginia	Charlottesville	Richmond	Seal
Pocahontas	Jefferson Davis	Judicial Branch	Atlantic Coastal Plain	Lewis and Clark
Appalachian Plateau	Tobacco		Yorktown	Shenandoah Valley
Mount Rogers	Robert E. Lee	James River	Piedmont	Pentagon
Chesapeake Bay	Motto	Mount Vernon	James Monroe	Monticello

Virginia Bingo

Patrick Henry	Tobacco	Cape Henry Lighthouse	Thomas Jefferson	Motto
CIA	Pentagon	Border(s)	Flag	Judicial Branch
Nickname	Union		Mount Vernon	County (-ies)
Chesapeake Bay	Nat Turner	Piedmont	Confederate States of America	Virginia Plan
Jamestown	Executive Branch	Legislative Branch	Powhatan	Norfolk

Virginia Bingo

Norfolk	George Washington	Pentagon	University of Virginia	Flag
County (-ies)	Williamsburg	Union	Powhatan	Atlantic Coastal Plain
Legislative Branch	Dogwood		Pocahontas	Richmond
Executive Branch	Border(s)	Lewis and Clark	Virginia Plan	Nickname
Tobacco	CIA	Appalachian Plateau	Jamestown	Jefferson Davis

Virginia Bingo

Chesapeake Bay	George Washington	James River	Pentagon	Pocahontas
Union	CIA	Tobacco	Flag	Shenandoah Valley
University of Virginia	Charlottesville		County (-ies)	Dogwood
Monticello	Piedmont	Jefferson Davis	Appalachian Plateau	Virginia Plan
Executive Branch	Robert E. Lee	Powhatan	Legislative Branch	Patrick Henry

Virginia Bingo

Confederate States of America	Union	Cape Henry Lighthouse	Flag	Chesapeake Bay
Jefferson Davis	Legislative Branch	Pentagon	Atlantic Coastal Plain	Tobacco
Thomas Jefferson	Yorktown		Mount Vernon	Border(s)
Robert E. Lee	Piedmont	Appalachian Plateau	Charlottesville	Jamestown
Executive Branch	Richmond	Shenandoah Valley	Motto	Monticello

Virginia Bingo

Patrick Henry	Flag	Cape Henry Lighthouse	Norfolk	University of Virginia
Thomas Jefferson	Mount Vernon	Judicial Branch	Union	Industry
Pocahontas	Legislative Branch		Nat Turner	Lewis and Clark
Executive Branch	Pentagon	CIA	Piedmont	Chesapeake Bay
Motto	James River	Powhatan	Seal	County (-ies)

Virginia Bingo

Charlottesville	Pentagon	CIA	Seal	John Smith
Richmond	Shenandoah Valley	Dogwood	Nickname	Yorktown
Chesapeake Bay	George Washington		Pocahontas	County (-ies)
Roanoke Colony	Jefferson Davis	Executive Branch	Patrick Henry	Virginia Plan
Industry	West Virginia	Powhatan	Jamestown	Tobacco

Virginia

Bingo

Virginia Bingo

Chesapeake Bay	Valley and Ridge	Blue Ridge	Pentagon	Confederate States of America
Patrick Henry	Industry	Piedmont	Yorktown	Dogwood
Flag	Virginia Plan		West Virginia	CIA
James Monroe	Motto	Monticello	Cape Henry Lighthouse	Shenandoah Valley
Mount Rogers	Border(s)	Norfolk	University of Virginia	George Washington

Virginia Bingo

Lewis and Clark	Appalachian Plateau	Jefferson Davis	Industry	Richmond
Tobacco	Chesapeake Bay	Mount Rogers	Pocahontas	Thomas Jefferson
Flag	Shenandoah Valley		Patrick Henry	Seal
James Monroe	Judicial Branch	Piedmont	Virginia Plan	Mount Vernon
West Virginia	Pentagon	Cape Henry Lighthouse	Valley and Ridge	James River

Virginia Bingo

Pocahontas	Thomas Jefferson	Pentagon	CIA	Appalachian Plateau
Patrick Henry	University of Virginia	Seal	Norfolk	Yorktown
Valley and Ridge	Confederate States of America		Atlantic Coastal Plain	Lewis and Clark
Mount Vernon	West Virginia	Mount Rogers	Blue Ridge	Border(s)
Nat Turner	John Smith	Motto	Monticello	Powhatan

Virginia Bingo

Appalachian Plateau	Valley and Ridge	University of Virginia	Pentagon	Atlantic Coastal Plain
Charlottesville	County (-ies)	Nickname	Mount Rogers	Richmond
George Washington	Dogwood		Roanoke Colony	Judicial Branch
James Monroe	Monticello	James River	Patrick Henry	West Virginia
James Madison	Williamsburg	John Smith	Virginia Plan	Thomas Jefferson

Virginia Bingo

Thomas Jefferson	Patrick Henry	Nickname	Pentagon	Robert E. Lee
George Washington	Blue Ridge	Jefferson Davis	CIA	Legislative Branch
Shenandoah Valley	Motto		Valley and Ridge	Cape Henry Lighthouse
Mount Rogers	Norfolk	West Virginia	James Monroe	Monticello
Roanoke Colony	John Smith	Powhatan	Chesapeake Bay	James River

Virginia Bingo

Nat Turner	Mount Vernon	Blue Ridge	Union	Chesapeake Bay
Richmond	University of Virginia	Lewis and Clark	CIA	Atlantic Coastal Plain
Jefferson Davis	Yorktown		Legislative Branch	Dogwood
West Virginia	James Monroe	Thomas Jefferson	Judicial Branch	Confederate States of America
John Smith	Patrick Henry	Valley and Ridge	Shenandoah Valley	Nickname

Virginia Bingo

Charlottesville	Valley and Ridge	Norfolk	Union	Powhatan
Industry	Appalachian Plateau	Motto	Blue Ridge	Judicial Branch
Mount Vernon	Chesapeake Bay		Atlantic Coastal Plain	Legislative Branch
Shenandoah Valley	John Smith	West Virginia	Patrick Henry	James River
Robert E. Lee	Monticello	Williamsburg	Mount Rogers	Thomas Jefferson

Virginia Bingo

			Valley and Ridge	Charlottesville
Richmond	Blue Ridge	Motto	Republican Party	Industry
Legislative Branch	Atlantic Coastal Plain		Chesapeake Bay	Mount Vernon
James River	Patrick Henry	West Virginia	John Smith	Shenandoah Valley
Thomas Jefferson	Mount Rogers	Williamsburg	Monticello	Robert E. Lee

Virginia Bingo

Charlottesville	Appalachian Plateau	Confederate States of America	Valley and Ridge	CIA
Pocahontas	Powhatan	Nickname	Richmond	Legislative Branch
Dogwood	Seal		Chesapeake Bay	Shenandoah Valley
Robert E. Lee	Border(s)	West Virginia	Blue Ridge	George Washington
James Madison	Roanoke Colony	John Smith	University of Virginia	Williamsburg

Virginia Bingo

Roanoke Colony	Nickname	Valley and Ridge	Cape Henry Lighthouse	Patrick Henry
Judicial Branch	Robert E. Lee	Blue Ridge	Charlottesville	Atlantic Coastal Plain
George Washington	CIA		Thomas Jefferson	West Virginia
Seal	James Monroe	Williamsburg	John Smith	Yorktown
Powhatan	Confederate States of America	Jefferson Davis	Industry	James Madison

Virginia Bingo

Border(s)	Valley and Ridge	James River	Richmond	Seal
Mount Rogers	University of Virginia	CIA	Appalachian Plateau	Charlottesville
Robert E. Lee	Mount Vernon		Yorktown	Roanoke Colony
Chesapeake Bay	Union	James Monroe	John Smith	West Virginia
Dogwood	Industry	Cape Henry Lighthouse	Williamsburg	James Madison

Virginia Bingo

James River	Jefferson Davis	Valley and Ridge	Appalachian Plateau	County (-ies)
Robert E. Lee	Mount Vernon	Blue Ridge	West Virginia	Atlantic Coastal Plain
Piedmont	Williamsburg		John Smith	Roanoke Colony
Seal	Thomas Jefferson	Nickname	James Madison	Judicial Branch
Chesapeake Bay	Yorktown	Border(s)	Nat Turner	Dogwood

Virginia Bingo

Pocahontas	Appalachian Plateau	Virginia Plan	Valley and Ridge	Jefferson Davis
County (-ies)	Border(s)	James River	Mount Rogers	Yorktown
Williamsburg	Shenandoah Valley		Seal	Richmond
Dogwood	Nat Turner	Motto	John Smith	West Virginia
Union	Flag	Chesapeake Bay	James Madison	Robert E. Lee

Virginia Bingo

James River	Appalachian Plateau	Seal	Industry	Flag
Robert E. Lee	Mount Rogers	Nickname	Dogwood	Nat Turner
George Washington	Border(s)		Atlantic Coastal Plain	Valley and Ridge
County (-ies)	James Monroe	Lewis and Clark	John Smith	West Virginia
Charlottesville	CIA	James Madison	Blue Ridge	Williamsburg

Virginia Bingo

Virginia Bingo

Confederate States of America	Valley and Ridge	Richmond	Flag	George Washington
Judicial Branch	Seal	Mount Vernon	Yorktown	Jamestown
James Madison	Patrick Henry		Dogwood	Nickname
Robert E. Lee	Blue Ridge	Appalachian Plateau	John Smith	Industry
James Monroe	Norfolk	Williamsburg	Border(s)	Lewis and Clark

Virginia Bingo: Card No. 30